For

NOAH'S ARK

RETOLD BY
Solomon M. Skolnick

ILLUSTRATED BY
Jo Gershman

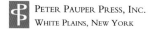

PETER PAUPER PRESS, INC.
WHITE PLAINS, NEW YORK

For Linda, Sophia, and Jesse

Copyright © 1996
Peter Pauper Press, Inc.
202 Mamaroneck Avenue
White Plains, NY 10601
ISBN 0-88088-802-4

Book design by Mullen & Katz

Printed in China

7 6 5 4 3

NOAH'S ARK

INTRODUCTION

The story of a great flood and its aftermath has made its way to us through the generations in diverse cultures and numerous languages.

The Biblical story of Noah and his family endures because it exemplifies redemption and renewal brought about through adherence to a moral code, the practice of faith, and the nurturing of hope.

—S.M.S.

In a place and time that is still vivid within our memories people acted with contempt toward each other, and toward the higher order that had set the earth into motion and provided its abundance.

God grieved for the
corruption that He saw.

He determined that the people who lived on the earth were beyond redemption, and set about to put an end to their days.

In that time a man
called Noah, and his wife,
lived in accord with the land
and followed the word of their
God. They had three sons,
each loyal in love and action
to their wives, their brothers,
and their own parents.

Ignoring the chaos around him,
Noah followed the one path
that he had promised to honor.

In time the voice of God
came to Noah.

God told Noah that the waters would swell the seas, fill the sky, and cover the earth, but that he and his family would be spared.

God instructed Noah to
build an ark on dry land.

Noah cleared a portion
of his fields. And in that clearing
he built an ark of cypress wood.
The vessel spanned 450 feet
from its bow to its stern.
Its width was 75 feet and
the peak of its roof reached
to 45 feet high.

A window with a view
to the heavens was crafted.
And doors that swung out from
the side of the ark were crafted.
All of the planks that formed
the ship were sealed from
within and without.

In each level of the great vessel
the family built rooms and
partitions, providing stalls and
bedding places for animals,
fowl, and themselves.

The ark was stocked with
provisions and food that
could be kept for a great
length of time.

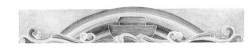

When the ark was
completed, Noah, his wife,
their sons and their families
boarded the sanctuary.

And a call went out.

Animals of every kind came
two by two, male and female,
in answer to the call.

Animals waking from their sleep stirred from their caves. Creatures of every kind came: those that sleep by day and prowl by night, those that favor the shade of the trees, and those that find sanctuary in the branches above.

Animals came to the ark:
those that intimidate by
creating loud noises and those
that surprise their prey
by stealth, those that graze
in open fields, and those that
draw fish from the river.

Animals of every kind
found safety in the great vessel.

Birds of every kind came
two by two, male and female,
in answer to the call.

Birds came to the ark:
those that are treasured for the
sweetness of their song, and
those that announce themselves
with a shriek, birds that soar
and birds that hover, and birds
that cannot take flight.

Birds came to the ark:
birds with great bills, and
those that peck with an
imperceptible motion,
birds with feathers as white
as the dove, and those
with feathers as black as
the raven.

Birds of every kind
found a nesting place
in the ark.

Seven days after all living
creatures were within the ark,
a wave of impenetrable clouds
moved to block the light of
the sun—turning day
into night.

The clouds swirled,
curling thickly and thundering
loudly, until the rain tore
through them with
a celestial rage.

And the rains came.

And it rained . . .

It rained for forty days
and forty nights.

The lakes, the rivers,
and the seas exploded with
turbulent spouts, sending their
waters up to meet the rain.

The waters covered
the flatlands that had been in
the shadow of the high hills.
The waters covered the
high hills that had been in the
shadow of the mountains.

The waters covered
the mountains that had been in
the shadow of the heavens.

Only the ark and its
inhabitants rose with the waters.

All save those in the ark
perished beneath the
rising waters.

The waters inundated the earth
for one hundred and fifty days.

And in time God blew a fair wind over the earth, causing the rain to cease and the turbulent waters to become calm.

The waters moved back
and back with a steady tide,
for one hundred and fifty days.

On the seventeenth day
of the seventh month the ark
came to rest on the
mountains of Ararat.

And the waters
continued to recede.

On the first day of the
tenth month the peaks of
the mountains, that had been
in the shadow of the heavens,
could be seen again.

After forty days on the
mountain of Ararat,
Noah opened the window that
he had crafted.

Through this window he
released a single raven.

And through this window he released a single dove.

The raven flew across
the face of the waters and
did not return.

The dove, unable to find a
dry place to set itself down,
returned to the ark.
Noah brought the dove inside
to the shelter of the ark.

Seven days passed.

Noah again released the single dove through the window that he had crafted.

The dove returned with
an olive branch and leaf
in its mouth.

Noah took the olive branch
with its leaf as a sign that waters
no longer covered the earth.

Seven more days passed and
Noah released the dove again.
This time the dove
did not return.

Noah opened wide the
doors of the ark, and the land
that he saw was dry.

And God told Noah to
come out of the ark that had
been his sanctuary.

Noah led his family,
and every living creature,
great and small, out through
the doors of the vessel.

Animals and birds of
every kind went two by two,
male and female,
onto the dry land.

Every animal and beast
went out from the ark
so that they might return to
the land and multiply.

And Noah built an altar.
The scent from the altar was
sweet to God.

And He blessed Noah,
and his wife, and his sons
and their wives.

God promised that day
would follow night, and night
would follow day, so that each
day in its turn would come.

And every season would come in its turn, one after another, so that seed could be planted and food harvested.

And God said to the
children of Noah: be fruitful
and replenish the earth.

God established His covenant
with Noah for his generation
and the generations to follow.

The covenant was sealed.
God would never again
flood the land and destroy
all living things.

God split the light
into its colors.

And He placed the colors
in a bow across the sky.

And God said that
each time there was rain,
and a cloud in the sky, the bow
would follow as a sign that
a covenant had been made
between God and
all humankind.

A man who trims
himself to suit
everybody will soon whittle
himself away.

Charles Schwab

Other
Health Communications Books
by Bryan E. Robinson

Work Addiction
Hidden Legacies Of Adult Children

Soothing Moments
Daily Meditations For Fast-Track Living

Heal Your Self—Esteem
Recovery From Addictive Thinking

Stressed Out?
A Guidebook For Taking Care Of Yourself

Healograms: Series 1
Healograms: Series 2
Healograms: Series 3

Overdoing It
How To Slow Down And
Take Care Of Yourself

MESSAGES FOR HEALTHY LIVING

HEALOGRAMS
2

HOW TO
TAKE CHARGE OF
YOUR LIFE

Bryan E. Robinson, Ph.D.
Jamey McCullers, R.N.

Health Communications, Inc.
Deerfield Beach, Florida

©1993 Bryan E. Robinson and
Jamey McCullers
ISBN 1-55874-284-0

Publisher: Health Communications, Inc.
3201 S.W. 15th Street
Deerfield Beach, FL 33442-8190

Graphic design by Graphic Expression
Color design by Barbara M. Bergman

INTRODUCTION
How To Take
Charge Of Your Life

Many of us are so accustomed to pleasing others and doing what is expected that we lose touch with our own lives. We may no longer know what we enjoy, what we want or what we need to do.

These *Healograms* — positive, healthy messages we send ourselves — help us more closely examine *our* lives. Are we leading them? Or are they leading us?

We learn who's in charge and how to reclaim the lead in our lives rather than letting someone make our choices for us.

We are not helpless pawns of fate, and no one else is responsible for how we feel or what we do. The gentle affirmations in this little book will help you find out whether or not you are giving your power away to others in your daily life. If you are, they will show you how to take charge of your life and move from spiritual adolescence to spiritual maturity as you become responsible for your feelings and actions.

Reflect on each message and silently apply it to your life. You will become actively involved in your own healing process as you write your own *Healograms* in the spaces provided.

Using *Healograms* as a guide, you will learn how to reclaim your life and watch it start to improve. If you want to enrich your life by feeling more in charge and by exercising all the choices available to you, these *Healograms* will show you how.

HEALOGRAMS are positive messages we send to ourselves to guide us through the day.

Part of taking charge of our lives is letting go of other people's opinions and living our lives to suit our own requirements.

How To Take Charge Of Your Life

1

Being Our Own Person

Sometimes we feel that if someone leaves us, there will be nothing left of us. We think we must
have someone else in order to
feel complete and worthy. Once
we start to know and value who
we are and to love and care for
ourselves, we feel complete with
the knowledge that we are never
alone because we have ourselves.

Each day of becoming our own

person brings us closer to our true selves. We know what we prefer instead of letting others tell us. We feel our own feelings, make our own decisions and stand up for what we believe without compromise. We enjoy our own company and march to the beat of our own drum, not someone else's. The following affirmation can help: *Today I will be my own person, cooperative and kind, but genuinely me. I will think, feel and do what feels right and healthy.*

*O*nce we start to know and value who we are and to love and care for ourselves, we feel complete just as we are and we need never feel alone again.

Bouncing Back

Sometimes we fall into old habits that we thought we had overcome and we feel as if we're right back where we started. But we're not. Sometimes it gets worse before it gets better. We might have to take three steps backward before leaping ten steps forward. Falling down is a necessary part of bouncing back.

It's not how far you fall, it's

how high you bounce back that counts. Temporary delays and roadblocks are a natural part of life's journey and a necessary part of our trip. When we face occasional barricades, we don't have to give up; there is always a new path to take. When life sets up roadblocks, we can look and wait for a detour to take us forward. Instead of throwing in the towel, we can accept the lows with the highs.

When life sets up roadblocks, we can look and wait for a detour to take us forward again.

3

Drawing The Line

A colleague asks us to do something we don't want to do and we say no. We speak up when a friend tries to take advantage of our good nature. We refuse to bail a loved one out of trouble for the umpteenth time. Sometimes the best way to care is to draw the line with our emotional involvement. Fixing someone's problem robs him of the benefit of doing it on his own.

The difference between caring for others and making ourselves a doormat is knowing where to draw the line. We can draw a line by letting others care for themselves and spending our time caring for our own neglected lives. We can learn to feel our own feelings, not someone else's, and allow others to experience the outcomes of their actions, instead of trying to save them from the consequences. Drawing the line can be one of the best gifts we give another person and ourselves.

The difference between caring for others and making ourselves a doormat is knowing where to draw the line; this can be one of the best gifts we give another person and ourselves.

4

Taking Life
As It Comes

When our lives are not going the way we want, we must remember that we cannot change ourselves overnight. It took us a long time to get where we are, and it will take time to undo the things we want to change.

A little patience and faith go a long way toward helping us get to where we want to be. For now we can take one step at a time.

We need take only this second,
this moment, this hour, this day.
We live our lives in the present
and make it through each day,
one by one. We give ourselves
credit for the tiny gains we make,
knowing that small steps add up
to giant strides. No matter how
hard life gets, we are comforted
in the simple reminder, *"One step
at a time."*

When our lives are not improving fast enough, we can remember to give ourselves credit for the tiny gains we make, knowing that small steps add up to giant strides.

Freeing Ourselves

When we believe we are inferior or unworthy, we imprison ourselves. Constantly putting ourselves down, shaming ourselves, putting ourselves last or doing what others want are additional bars on the prison cell we build around us.

Feelings of self-worth come from within. We must believe we count for something. Once we feel we are worthy of respect, other people will treat us with respect too. Freeing ourselves from our negative attitudes allows us to live our lives to the fullest.

We don't have to make ourselves inferior to others. We can care for and love ourselves so that we are on an equal plane with others. Once we begin to love and care for ourselves, others will love and care for us too.

*O*nce we begin to love and care for ourselves, others will love and care for us too.

6

Giving Ourselves Limits

Every day we hear about some tragedy and it grips our heart. Death and suffering are as much a part of life as love and joy. We can remember it is okay for us to have empathy for the victims but we must leave the emotions with them where they belong. It is important for us to remember to feel *with* others but not *for* them.

Life will always continue to

play out dramas. We can watch and be affected, but we do not have to be actors in someone else's drama. By remembering this, we can keep our focus on the part we have to play in our own lives, while loving and supporting others in theirs.

It is important to have empathy for others, but it is equally important for us to feel **with** *them, not* **for** *them.*

7

Accepting All Situations

We use the labels "bad" and "good" to describe how our lives unfold. Sometimes the things we define as bad turn out to be our richest blessings. When the salesperson missed his flight, he cursed and screamed that he would miss his important business meeting. But when he heard that the plane had crashed, the meeting no longer seemed important and he fell to his knees and gave thanks for his life.

It is impossible for us to know which outcomes are the best for us. Knowing that our well-being is in the hands of our Higher Power allows us to accept every situation at face value, without labeling it "good" or "bad." Once we learn that things happen as they are supposed to happen, we learn to accept all situations.

*O*nce we learn that things happen as they are supposed to happen, we learn to accept all situations and look for the message to be learned instead of labeling it as "good" or "bad."

8

Paddling Our Own Canoe

When we are aggressive, we steamroll over others who disagree or behave differently. When we are passive, we let others thrust their needs and rights upon us. These are two extreme actions on opposite ends of a continuum.

There is a middle ground that puts us more in charge of our lives. When we feel that we count for something and start standing up for ourselves, instead of seeking power over others or allowing someone else to dominate us, we can state our beliefs, feelings and desires without depriving others of their rights or letting them deprive us of ours.

We take charge of our lives when we start believing that we count for something and start standing up for ourselves.

9

Overcoming Emotional Paralysis

Do you find yourself floundering on important decisions that are eventually made by someone else or by chance? Taking action and making sound decisions is a big part of our responsibility to ourselves. When we leave decision-making to someone else, we lose control of our lives and make ourselves victims. No matter how boxed in we feel, there's always

33

some action we can take.

The way to reclaim control of our lives is to take action on matters we have left to chance. Today let's ask ourselves what things we can do that we usually leave to other people.

The way we reclaim control of our lives is to take action on matters we have left to chance.

10

Developing A Positive Image

For most of our lives we believe the lies: that we are stupid, unattractive and inadequate; that the world is full of crises, misery and suffering. Growing up we learned to see the world and ourselves as it was shown to us through the eyes of grown-ups. These well-intentioned adults, who did the best they could with their own problems, often mirrored the negative instead of the positive aspects. Once grown, we begin to view things the same way.

We can reframe our mirrors of the past. We can look back and examine the people who mirrored those negative images to us. We will see that things were not that way at all. We can learn to recast the old mirrors in terms of our own beauty and the universal human good, and we can begin to reflect the same to others.

As we reframe our negative images of the past in terms of our own beauty and the universal human good, we begin to reflect the same to others.

11

Overcoming People-Pleasing

Why is what others think so important to us? Some of us go to such lengths to please others that we forget who we are and what we want. Living our lives by what others think puts them in charge of our lives. With people-pleasing, our personalities change with whoever is around us. We lose self-respect and others lose respect for us because we cannot take a stand.

Overcoming people-pleasing allows us to live our lives according to what's right for us, not someone else. We accomplish this by standing firm on who we are and what we believe in. We earn the respect of others but, more importantly, we keep our own self-respect.

Part of taking charge of our lives is letting go of other people's opinions and living our lives to suit ourselves.

12

Being More Flexible

Some of us waste so much time and energy trying to be in control that we create disappointments for ourselves. Sometimes our lives are so out of control we feel like a trapeze artist flying through space.

There is a difference between being in charge and being in control. When we're in charge, we're flexible and willing to bend.

When we're in control, we're rigid and inflexible and unable to roll with the punches. Being in charge takes the form of delegating, brainstorming and creative problem-solving. Being in control takes the form of dictating, ordering and unilateral decision-making. Holding on, while making us feel in control, closes us down and imprisons us. Letting go opens us up, frees us and puts us in charge.

As we examine the parts of our lives that we compulsively control, we can gradually free ourselves by being willing to bend once in a while so that we do not break.

13

Becoming More Adult

Three parts make up our personalities: the child, the parent and adult. Many of us feel vulnerable and afraid. We feel childlike inside. Perhaps we feel like crying when someone snaps at us, feel panic-stricken when a close friend moves away or feel like having a temper tantrum when things don't go our way. When we experience these helpless feelings of the child, we forget that we are competent adults.

When we judge and criticize ourselves through guilt and shame, the parent part of us is in charge. The nurturing adult part of us helps to soothe the fears of the child and stands up to the ridiculing voice of the parent. By putting our adult in charge, we can challenge the critical parent and protect the vulnerable child. Our mature adult can find comfort and security that will satisfy all of our needs.

By putting the adult part of ourselves in charge, we can stand up to the critical parent and protect the vulnerable child part of ourselves.

14

Changing Ourselves

Many of us waste enormous amounts of energy trying to get others to be different — to be like we want them to be. Nothing we do can change someone else. We have about as much chance of changing others as we do of getting a tree to fly. The best thing we can do is leave them alone and put our energy into changing ourselves.

The only way we can make a difference in others is to do something different ourselves. As we begin to behave differently from our usual pattern, others will begin to behave differently toward us. The only way we can get others to change is to change ourselves first. Everything begins with us and flows from that.

The only way to get others to change is to change ourselves first.

15

Putting Forth Effort

Many times we become so paralyzed by the task ahead of us that we cannot gather the strength and momentum to start improving our lives. We hem and haw, make excuses and waste time and energy in order to avoid taking charge.

But once we can start the momentum, it carries us forward — clearing all the obstacles one step at a time until the task is finished. Looking back at the process, we remind ourselves that we actually did take charge and improve our lives.

It takes mental effort to change our lives and make them what we want them to be. Louise Hay suggests that each of us ask ourselves this question: "How much mental effort are you willing to exert to change your life and make it the life you want?"

It takes mental effort to change our lives and make them what we want.

Healograms

Series 1

1. How To Take Care Of Yourself
2. How To Live Your Life To The Fullest
3. How To Resolve The Conflict In Your Life
4. How To Make Your Life A Miracle

Series 2

1. How To Feel Good In Relationships
2. How To Learn To Love Yourself

Available in bookstores or by
calling 1-800-441-5569
Health Communications, Inc.